Correspondence Between The President And General Joseph E. Johnston, Together With That Of The Secretary Of War And The Adjutant And Inspector General, During The Months Of May, June And July, 1863

Confederate States Of America. President

Nabu Public Domain Reprints:

You are holding a reproduction of an original work published before 1923 that is in the public domain in the United States of America, and possibly other countries. You may freely copy and distribute this work as no entity (individual or corporate) has a copyright on the body of the work. This book may contain prior copyright references, and library stamps (as most of these works were scanned from library copies). These have been scanned and retained as part of the historical artifact.

This book may have occasional imperfections such as missing or blurred pages, poor pictures, errant marks, etc. that were either part of the original artifact, or were introduced by the scanning process. We believe this work is culturally important, and despite the imperfections, have elected to bring it back into print as part of our continuing commitment to the preservation of printed works worldwide. We appreciate your understanding of the imperfections in the preservation process, and hope you enjoy this valuable book.

CORRESPONDENCE

BETWEEN

THE PRESIDENT

AND

GENERAL JOSEPH E. JOHNSTON,

TOGETHER WITH THAT OF

THE SECRETARY OF WAR AND THE ADJUTANT AND INSPECTOR GENERAL,

DURING THE MONTHS OF MAY, JUNE AND JULY, 1863.

PUBLISHED BY ORDER OF CONGRESS.

RICHMOND:
R. M. SMITH, PUBLIC PRINTER.
1864.

MESSAGE OF THE PRESIDENT.

RICHMOND, Va., January 29, 1864.

To the House of Representatives:

In response to your resolution of the 11th ultimo, I herewith transmit for your information a copy of my correspondence, together with that of the Secretary of War and of the Adjutant and Inspector General, with General Joseph E. Johnston, during the months of May, June, and July, 1863, concerning his command and the operations in his department."

As the resolution fixes definitely the dates within which the correspondence is desired, I have not deemed it proper to add anything which was prior or subsequent to those dates.

JEFFERSON DAVIS.

CORRESPONDENCE

BETWEEN

THE PRESIDENT AND GEN. JOHNSTON.

TELEGRAM.

RICHMOND, Va., May 6, 1863.

Gen. J. E. JOHNSTON, *Tullahoma, Tenn.:*

How and why was Brigadier General Martin withdrawn from Mississippi, for service with the cavalry of which he was appointed?

(Signed)   JEFFERSON DAVIS.

TELEGRAM.

TULLAHOMA, TENN., May 7, 1863.

His Excellency, the President:

Brigadier General Martin was assigned to Van Dorn's cavalry, which was ordered to this department in January. He is not now with Van Dorn, who is in front of Columbia. He commands the cavalry directly between this army and Murfreesboro.'

(Signed.)   J. E. JOHNSTON.

TELEGRAM IN CYPHER.

RICHMOND, May 18, 1863.

General JOSEPH E. JOHNSTON,
    Headquarters, via Jackson, Miss.:

Have seen your despatch of this date. The cavalry mentioned cannot reach you before weeks. Other larger and more practised cavalry I had hoped could be drawn to you from another part of your department, as suggested in telegram some time since. Several of the best infantry regiments, if wanted, might serve as substitute for the cavalry so much and immediately required. I hope you will have larger accessions to your army, when advancing to attack, by the junction of militia and less organized bodies of citizens. Your presence will effect much to inspire confidence and activity.

The enemy will probably seek to join his fleet at Warrenton, draw the remaining forces from the camp above Young's Point, and prepare for land and water attack on the defences of Vicksburg. If you could unite with Pemberton, and attack the enemy in his retrograde movement towards the river, the chances would be much better. Every effort will be made to aid you, and I desire to know fully your wishes.

 (Signed)   JEFFERSON DAVIS.

TELEGRAM.

CANTON, May 21, 1863.

To his Excellency, the President:

There is a divison without a Major General, the only officer competent to command it being General W. H. T. Walker;* (he) is the junior Brigadier. Please appoint immediately. Another will be wanted for coming troops. I recommend Brig. Gen. Wilcox.* These officers are indispensable.

 (Signed)   J. E. JOHNSTON.

TELEGRAM.

CAMP NEAR CANTON, *via Jackson,* May 21, 1863.

To the President:

Your dispatch of the 18th received, but cannot be decyphered. On account of heavy loss of artillery, we want field-pieces, with harness and ammunition. Troops coming from the east are generally without artillery.

 (Signed)   J. E. JOHNSTON.

COPY OF TELEGRAM.

RICHMOND, VA., May 22, 1863.

General Jos. E. Johnston, via Jackson, Miss.:

Brigadier General John S. Bowen is appointed Major General to meet the want specified in your dispatch. General Loring becomes available for assignment to the division you designate. Field batte-

---

* These names, in the original dispatch received, appeared as "General W. H. Taliaferro," and "Brigadier General Wilson."

ries and small arms are on the way to your command. Signal cypher was employed. If you have the book formerly used by us, will resort to that.

    (Signed)   JEFFERSON DAVIS.

COPY OF TELEGRAM.

RICHMOND, May 22, 1863.

General BRAGG, *Tullahoma, Tenn.:*

The vital issue of holding the Mississippi at Vicksburg is dependent on the success of General Johnston in an attack on the investing force. The intelligence from there is discouraging. Can you aid him? If so, and you are without orders from General Johnston, act on your judgment.

    (Signed)   JEFFERSON DAVIS.

TELEGRAM.

RICHMOND, May 22, 1863.

General Jos. E. JOHNSTON, *via Jackson, Miss.:*

I do not understand recommendation for promotion of Brigadier General Wilson, in your despatch of 21st.

    (Signed)   JEFFERSON DAVIS.

TELEGRAM.

JACKSON, Miss., May 23, 1863.

His Excellency, the President:

It was Brigadier General Cadmus Wilcox that I recommended. Major General Loring is commanding his own division. Brigadier General Bowen commands a division of the troops invested in Vicksburg. The division I mentioned has no officer in it competent to command but Brigadier General W. H. T. Walker. It must be without a commander until a Major General is appointed for or assigned to it.

We have tremendous odds against us. I respectfully urge, therefore, thorough organization.

I ceased to carry the book referred to upon being informed that the copy was not retained in your office.

The enemy's gunboats have possession of the Yazoo.

    (Signed)   J. E. JOHNSTON.

TELEGRAM.

SHELBYVILLE, TENN., May 23, 1863.

JEFFERSON DAVIS, *President:*

Sent thirty-five hundred (3,500) with the General, three (3) batteries of artillery and two thousand (2,000) cavalry since; will despatch six thousand (6,000) more immediately. Have no orders. The General did not consider it safe to weaken this point.

(Signed)   BRAXTON BRAGG.

TELEGRAM.

RICHMOND, VA., May 23, 1863.

General B. BRAGG, *commanding, &c., Shelbyville, Tenn.:*

Your answer is in the spirit of patriotism heretofore manifested by you. The need is sore, but you must not forget your own necessities.

(Signed)   JEFFERSON DAVIS.

TELEGRAM.

RICHMOND, VA., May 23, 1863.

To General J. E. JOHNSTON, *via Canton, Miss.:*

Your first dispatch was so changed as to present the names of W. H. Taliaferro and Wilson—both supposed to be errors. Bowen was appointed supposing him to be with Loring. Since your dispatch received to-day, gave order to appoint Walker Major General. Am making every effort to aid you, and hopeful of junction of your forces and defeat of the enemy.

(Signed)   JEFFERSON DAVIS.

TELEGRAM.

JACKSON, MISS., May 23, 1863.

To his Excellency, the President:

Troops are coming very slowly. The last of Bragg's arrived on Tuesday; since then but three hundred have arrived, and thirteen hundred are reported this side of Meridian. An officer who left Vicksburg on Tuesday reports that an assault near the Yazoo road had been repelled this time. It is said here to-day that another was made near the Jackson road, and also repulsed. This gives me confidence in Pemberton's tenacity. If army can be organized, and well commanded, we shall win.

Major Generals in proportion to the number of brigades are necessary. Is Major General Ewell assigned? I have great confidence in him, and should be glad to have him.

(Signed)   J. E. JOHNSTON.

TELEGRAM IN CYPHER.

JACKSON, May 23, 1863.

To the President:

The number of troops I expect to concentrate now in Mississippi is nineteen (19) thousand, exclusive of the garrison of Vicksburg and Port Hudson. The latter I have ordered to join me. Vicksburg is invested. Number sixteen (16) thousand or eighteen (18) thousand. Grant's force is estimated at sixty thousand (60,000.)

(Signed)   J. E. JOHNSTON.

TELEGRAM IN CYPHER.

CANTON, May 24th, 1863.

To His Excellency the President:

The following, received by courier, at Jackson, yesterday, from General Pemberton, telegraphed to me by Colonel Ewell:

"VICKSBURG, May 20th.—Enemy assaulted entrenchments yesterday on centre and left. Were repulsed with heavy loss. Our loss small. Enemy's force at least sixty (60) thousand.

"MAY 21ST.—Enemy kept up heavy artillery fire yesterday. Two (2) guns dismounted in centre, and works uninjured. Their sharpshooters picked off officers and men all day. Works repaired and guns replaced last night. The vital (U S R R A) question is ammunition.

"The men are encouraged by a report that you are near with a large army, and are in good spirits.

"Two, P. M.—Brisk artillery and musketry fire to-day. Three (3) guns dismounted in centre; will replace them if possible. Heavy mortar firing from gunboats. The fire of the sharpshooters is severe.

"THREE O'CLOCK, P. M.—During past two days enemy has gone up river in transports in large force. Where going, not known."

(Signed,)   JOS. E. JOHNSTON.

TELEGRAM.

RICHMOND, May 24th, 1863.

To General J. E. JOHNSTON, *Canton, Miss.*:

I concur in your reliance on the tenacity with which General Pemberton will defend his position, but the desparity of numbers renders prolonged defence dangerous. I hope you will soon be able to break the investment, make a juncture, and carry in munitions. General Rains, who has made valuable inventions, is ordered to you for special service, and will, I think, be useful both on land and river. Gen'l Bragg has probably communicated with you. If my strength permitted, I would go to you.

(Signed,) JEFFERSON DAVIS.

TELEGRAM IN CYPHER.

JACKSON, May 27th, 1863.

To His Excellency, the President:

A young man, sent out by Major General Stevenson, reports that hard fighting has been going on since Tuesday of last week, with continued success to us. Our men confident and in fine spirits; but we cannot break the investment without an army. General Cooper tells me that but thirteen (13) thousand have been ordered. General Pemberton estimates Grant's force at not less than sixty (60) thousand. When all the reinforcements arrive, shall have but twenty-three (23) thousand. Tell me if additional troops can be furnished.

The two cases of cypher are independent of each other.

(Signed,) J. E. JOHNSTON.

TELEGRAM IN CYPHER.

RICHMOND, May 28th, 1863.

To General J. E. JOHNSTON, *Canton, Miss.*:

The reinforcements sent to you exceed by, say, seven thousand, the estimate of your dispatch of 27th instant. We have withheld nothing which it was practicable to give. We cannot hope for numerical equality, and time will probably increase the disparity.

(Signed,) JEFFERSON DAVIS.

TELEGRAM.

Jackson, May 28th, 1863.

To His Excellency, the President:

It is reported that the last infantry coming, leave Montgomery to-night. When they arrive I shall have about twenty-three thousand (23,000.) Pemberton can be saved only by beating Grant. Unless you can promise more troops we must try with that number. The odds against us will be very great. Can you not add seven thousand? Asked for another major general, Wilcox or whoever you may prefer. We want good general officers quickly. I have to organize an army and collect ammunition, provisions, and transportation.

(Signed,)   J. E. JOHNSTON.

TELEGRAM IN CYPHER.

Richmond, May 30th, 1863.

To General Jos. E. Johnston, Jackson, Miss.:

Your dispatch, of 28th, received. The Secretary of War reports the reinforcement ordered to you as greater than the number you request. Added to the forces you have from Pemberton's army, he states your whole force to be thirty-four (34) thousand, exclusive of militia. Bowen and Walker promoted. French and Breckinridge, ordered to you, will, I hope, meet your want of major generals. If another be required, S. D. Lee is, I think, equal to that grade. Officers in the field here cannot be sent to you without too great delay. The troops sent to you were so fully organized that I suppose you will have little trouble as to organization, unless it be of militia. Colonel Stockton can probably answer your requisitions for ammunition. You, no doubt, will be embarrassed by deficiency of field transportation. The recent robberies have diminished the amount in the country.

(Signed,)   JEFFERSON DAVIS.

TELEGRAM IN CYPHER.

Canton, June 1, 1863, *via Montgomery, 2d.*

To his Excellency, the President:

The Secretary of War is greatly mistaken in his numbers. By

their own returns, the troops at my disposal available against Grant are:

Of Pemberton's	9,700
Of Bragg's	8,400
Of Beauregard's	6,000
	24,100

Not including a few hundred irregular cavalry nor Jackson's command, the strength of which I do not know. Bowen and Lee are in Vicksburg beyond my reach. In the estimate, that garrison is not included.

The total of the above, twenty-four thousand one hundred (24,100.) These are numbers of effectives.

(Signed,)   J. E. JOHNSTON.

TELEGRAM.

CANTON, *via Montgomery*, June 10, 1863.

To His Excellency, President Davis:

It has been suggested to me that the troops in this department are very hostile to officers of northern birth, and that, on that account, Major General French's arrival will weaken instead of strengthen us. I beg you to consider that all the general officers of northern birth are on duty in this department. There is now a want of major generals.

It is important to avoid any cause of further discontent.

(Signed,)   J. E. JOHNSTON.

TELEGRAM.

RICHMOND, VA., June 11, 1863.

To General JOSEPH E. JOHNSTON:

Your dispatch received. Those who suggest that the arrival of General French will produce discontent among the troops, because of his northern birth are not, probably, aware that he is a citizen of Mississippi, was a wealthy planter until the Yankees robbed him, and, before the Confederate States had an army, was the chief of ordnance and artillery in the force Mississippi raised to maintain her right of secession. As soon as Mississippi could spare him, he was appointed a brigadier general in the provisional army of the Confederate States, and has frequently been before the enemy, where he was the senior officer. If malignity should undermine him, as it has another, you are authorized to notify him of the fact and to relieve him, communicating it to me by telegram. Surprised by your remark as to the general officers of northern birth, I turned to the register and find that a large majority of the number are elsewhere than in the Department of Mississippi and eastern Louisiana.

(Signed,)   JEFFERSON DAVIS.

TELEGRAM.

JACKSON, June 12, 1863.

To Hon. J. A. SEDDON, *Secretary of War:*

Your dispatch of the 8th, imperfectly deciphered and partially answered on the tenth. I have not considered myself commanding in Tennessee since assignment here, and should have not felt authorized to take troops from that department after having been informed by the Executive that no more could be spared. To take from Bragg a force which would make this army fit to oppose Grant would involve yielding Tennessee. It is for the Government to decide between this State and Tennessee.

(Signed,)   J. E. JOHNSTON.

TELEGRAM.

RICHMOND, June 13, 1863.

To General BRAGG, *Tullahoma, Tenn.:*

General Johnston communicates report of reinforcements to Grant going down the Mississippi. The estimated number, thirty thousand. Have you knowledge whence they were drawn. If from Rosecranz, can you further aid the defence of Vicksburg, indirectly or directly, by advance or detachment?

(Signed,)   JEFFERSON DAVIS.

TELEGRAM.

RICHMOND, June 15, 1863.

To General J. E. JOHNSTON, *Jackson, Miss.:*

Your dispatch, of 12th instant, to Secretary of War, noted. The order to go to Mississippi did not diminish your authority in Tennessee, both being in the country placed under your command in original assignment. To what do you refer as information from me restricting your authority to transfer troops, because no more could be spared? Officers ordered to you for duty generally are, of course, subject to assignment by you.

(Signed,)   JEFFERSON DAVIS.

TELEGRAM.

JACKSON, June 15th, 1863.

To Hon. J. A. SEDDON, *Secretary of War:*

Your repeated dispatch of the 8th, is deciphered. I cannot advise in regard to the points from which troops can best be taken, having no means of knowing; nor is it for me to judge which it is best to yield, (or hold) Mississippi or Tennessee; that is for the Government to determine. Without some great blunder of the enemy, we cannot hold both. The odds against me are much greater than those you express. I consider saving Vicskburg hopeless.

(Signed,)   J. E. JOHNSTON.

TELEGRAM.

JACKON, June 16, 1863.

To His Excellency the President:

Your dispatch of 15th received. I meant to tell the Secretary of War that I considered the order directing me to command here as limiting (my) authority to this department, especially when that order was accompaned by War Department orders transferring troops from Tennessee to Mississippi; and, whether commanding there or not, that your reply to my application for more troops, that none could be spared, would have made it improper for me to order more from Tennessee. Permit me to repeat that an officer having a task like mine, far above his ability, cannot, in addition, command other remote departments. No general can command separate armies.

I have not yet been able to procure the means of moving these troops. They are too weak to accomplish much. The reinforcements you mention have joined Grant.

(Signed,)   J. E. JOHNSTON.

TELEGRAM.

JACKSON, June 16, 1863.

To Hon. J. A. SEDDON, *Secretary of War:*

General Bragg informs me that a telegram from Louisville, of the 10th, says that part of the ninth and third corps have been sent to reinforce Grant. Will not this enable us to *invade* Kentucky? For this General Bragg's command should extend over east Tennessee.

 (Signed,)
            J. E. JOHNSTON.

TELEGRAM.

RICHMOND, June 17, 1863.

To General J. E. JOHNSTON, *Jackson, Miss.*:

I do not find in my letter book any communication to you containing the expression which you again attribute to me, and cite as a restriction on you against withdrawing troops from Tennessee; and have to repeat my inquiry, to what do you refer? Give date of dispatch or letter.

 (Signed)
            JEFFERSON DAVIS.

RICHMOND, June 17, 1863.

To Gen. B. BRAGG, *commanding, &c., Shelbyville, Tenn.*:

GENERAL: Gen. Johnston, in telegrams of the 15th and 16th, repeats the expression of his opinion that he cannot, under existing circumstances, advantageously command both in Mississippi and Tennessee; and, in referring to the reported movement of Burnside's corps to reinforce Grant, says: "Will not this enable us to invade Kentucky? For this General Bragg's command should extend over east Tennessee.

The arrangement made of several departments, in a geographical district, to the command of which General Johnston was assigned, was intended to secure the fullest co-operation of the troops in those departments, and, at the same time, to avoid delay by putting the commander of each department in direct correspondence with the war office.

Under this view of the case, the department of east Tennessee, &c., was created because of the delay which would attend the transmission of reports and orders if they must need pass from southwestern Virginia to middle Tennessee, and thence to Richmond, Virginia. Your telegram of the 15th, suggesting orders for co-operative movement by General Buckner, manifests the defect of the existing arrangement, while General Johnston's attention is absorbed by operations in Mississippi.

I would be glad to have from you such suggestions as you may please to make in relation to the proper remedy for the existing evil.

Your command could be extended to embrace that of Gen. Buckner, by extending the limits of the department of Tennessee. You will know better than myself how far the means of communication and your own leisure would permit you to direct the operations, especially in the eastern portion of Gen. Buckners' department.

You can also judge better than myself how far co-operation can be relied upon, without the exercise of other command than that which arises after the junction of forces in camp, marches, &c.

There are, no doubt, many conditions which do not now occur to me, but which experience has brought to your attention, and I will be glad to have a full expression of your views, being happily fully aware that your wish can in no wise differ from my own, the success of our cause in the unequal struggle in which we are engaged.

Very respectfully and truly yours,
(Signed)   JEFFERSON DAVIS.

TELEGRAM.

JACKSON, June 20, 1863.

Hon. J. A. SEDDON, *Secretary of War*:

On arriving here I informed General Kirby Smith of the condition of Vicksburg and Port Hudson, and requested his aid and co-operation, which he has given.

General Taylor, with eight thousand men, is opposite Vicksburg, and temporarily occupies Milliken's Bend and other points on the river. The presence of this force is encouraging. Nothing can be done by us to relieve Port Hudson, which is in imminent peril. General Taylor will make such demonstrations opposite Port Hudson as he can.

(Signed)   J. E. JOHNSTON.

TELEGRAM.

JACKSON, June 20, 1863.

To His Excellency, the President:

I much regret the carelessness of my reply of the 16th, to your telegram of the 15th. In my dispatch of the 12th, to the Secretary of War, I referred to words "we have withheld nothing which it was practicable to give," in your telegram of May 28th, and (to the tele-

gram) of June 5th*, except the last sentence. I considered "Executive" as including Secretary of War.
(Signed) J. E. JOHNSTON.

TELEGRAM IN CYPHER.

RICHMOND, June 25, 1863.

To Gen. J. E. JOHNSTON, *Jackson, Miss.*:

Telegram from Governor Pettus informs me of conference with you. Com. Barron will transfer the funds to you, to be applied by you for the purpose indicated, in the defence of western rivers. You will exercise discretionary power as to manner and objects.
(Signed) JEFFERSON DAVIS.

TELEGRAM IN CYPHER.

JACKSON, *via Montgomery*, June 28, 1863.

His Excellency, the President:

I have received what you directed Commodore Barron to give me; but, since learning particulars of the scheme with which he was connected, have no hope now of * * * * * *

The third object seems to me feasible, and agents have been despatched * * * * * * * *

I shall probably not require a tenth part of the money.
(Signed) J. E. JOHNSTON

TELEGRAM.

RICHMOND, June 30, 1863.

To Gen. J. E. JOHNSTON, *Jackson, Miss.*:

After full examination of all correspondence between you and myself and the war office, including the dispatches referred to in your telegram of the 20th instant, I am still at a loss to account for your strange error in stating to the Secretary of War that your right to draw reinforcements from Bragg's army had been restricted by the Executive, or that your command over the army of Tennessee had been withdrawn.

In compliance with your request, I am engaged in correspondence with General Bragg on the subject of making such new arrangements

---
*From the Secretary of War.

as shall relieve you hereafter of the command of his department. Your suggestion to extend Bragg's command over east Tennessee, is likewise a subject of correspondence; and your recommendation to attempt a movement in Kentucky has been approved, and every effort will be made to carry into effect that as well as any other practicable movement to aid you.

(Signed,)   JEFFERSON DAVIS.

TELEGRAM.

RICHMOND, July 2, 1863.

To General J. E. JOHNSTON:

I have this day sent a dispatch to General E. K. Smith, and to your care. Please send copies of the dispatch to General Smith by several reliable couriers, going at different times, so as to ensure its speedy delivery.

(Signed,)   JEFFERSON DAVIS.

TELEGRAM.

HEADQUARTERS, CANEY CREEK, MADISON CO.,
July 4, 1863, *via Jackson.*

To His Excellency, President DAVIS:

Your dispatch of the 2d instant, received, but none of it can be deciphered. Please repeat.

(Signed,)   J. E. JOHNSTON.

TELEGRAM.

CANEY CREEK CAMP, July 5, 1863.

To his Excellency, the President:

Your dispatch of June 30th, received. I considered my assignment to the immediate command in Mississippi as giving me a new position and limiting my authority to this department. The orders of the War Department transferring three separate bodies of troops from General Bragg's army to this, two of them without my knowledge, and all of them, without consulting me, would have convinced me, had I doubted. These orders of the War Department expressed its judgment of the number of troops to be transferred from Tennessee; I could no more control this judgement by increasing the number than by forbidding the transfer. I regret very much that an impression which seemed to me to be natural, should be regarded by you as a strange error. I thank your Excellency for your approval of the several recommendations you mention.

 (Signed,)   J. E. JOHNSTON.

TELEGRAM.

JACKSON, July 7, 1863.

To Hon. J. A. SEDDON, *Secretary of War:*

Vicksburg capitulated on the 4th instant. Garrison was paroled, and are to be returned to our lines; the officers retaining their side arms and personal baggage. This intelligence was brought by an officer who left the place on Sunday the 5th. In consequence, I am falling back from the Big Black river to Jackson.

 (Signed,)   J. E. JOHNSTON, *General.*

TELEGRAM.

RICHMOND, July 8, 1863.

To General J. E. JOHNSTON, *Jackson, Mississippi:*

Your dispatch of 5th instant, received. The mistakes it contains will be noticed by letter. Your dispatch of 7th instant, to Secretary of War, announcing the disastrous termination of the siege of Vicksburg received same day.

Painfully anxious as to the result, I have remained without information from you as to any plans proposed or attempted to raise the siege. Equally uninformed, as to your plans in relation to Port Hudson. I have to request such information, in relation thereto, as the Government has a right to expect from one of its commanding generals in the field.

 (Signed,)   JEFFERSON DAVIS.

TELEGRAM.

JACKSON, July 9, 1863.

To *his Excellency, the President:*

Your dispatch of to-day* received. I have never meant to fail in the duty of reporting to the Executive, whatever might interest it in my

---

*Dated Richmond, July 8, 1863.

command. I informed the Secretary of War that my force was much too weak to attempt to raise the siege of Vicksburg, and that to attempt to relieve Port Hudson would be to give up Mississippi, as it would involve the loss of this point, and that the want of adequate means of transportation kept me inactive until the end of June. I then moved towards Vicksburg to attempt to extricate the garrison, but could not devise a plan until after reconnoitering, for which, I was too late. Without General Pemberton's co-opperation, any attempt must have resulted in disaster.

The slowness and difficulty of communication rendered co-operation next to impossible.

(Signed,) J. E. JOHNSTON.

TELEGRAM.

RICHMOND, July 9, 1863.

To General J. E. JOHNSTON, *Jackson, Mississippi:*

If it be true that General Taylor has joined General Gardner and routed Banks, you will endeavor to draw heavy reinforcements from that army, and delay a general engagement, until your junction is effected. Thus, it is to be hoped, the enemy may yet be crushed and the late disaster be repaired.

Send by telegraph a list of the general and staff officers who have come out on parole from Vicksburg, so that they may be exchanged immediately. As soon as practicable, let the lists of regiments and other organizations be forwarded, for same purpose. General Rains should now fully apply his invention.

(Signed,) JEFFERSON DAVIS.

TELEGRAM.

JACKSON, July 9, 1863.

To his Excellency, the President:

The enemy is advancing in two columns on Jackson, now about four miles distant. I shall endeavor to hold the place as the possession of Mississippi depends on it. His force is about double ours.

(Signed,) J. E. JOHNSTON, *General.*

TELEGRAM.

Jackson, July 10, 1863.

To his Excellency, President Davis:

Your dispatch of yesterday received. No report of Taylor's junction with Gardner has reached me, as it must have done, if true, as we have twelve hundred (1200) cavalry in that vicinity. I have nothing official from Vicksburg. Major Jacob Thompson, of General Pemberton's staff, gives me the following list: Lieutenant General Pemberton, Major Generals Stevenson, Forney, M. L. Smith and Bowen. Brigadier Generals Barton, Lee, Cumming, Moore, Hebert, Baldwin, Vaughan, Shoup. Colonels Reynolds, Waul and Cockerill, commanders brigades, also Brigadier General Harris, of Mississippi militia.

(Signed,) J. E. JOHNSTON.

TELEGRAM IN CYPHER.

Jackson, July 11, 1863.

To the President:

Under General Pemberton's orders, a line of rifle-pits was constructed from the Canton road at Colonel Withers' house, passing a few hundred yards from the railroad depot, and going to the New Orleans railroad, one thousand (1,000) yards south. It is very defective, cannot stand seige, but improves a bad position against assault. I thought want of water would compel this, but the enemy has made no attempt, but skirmished all day yesterday. Should he not assault, we must attack him or leave the place. Prisoners say these are Ord's and Sherman's corps, and three other divisions. Their right is near Raymond road, their left on Pearl river opposite insane asylum. Our men are deserting in large numbers by the fords on Pearl river.

(Signed,) J. E. JOHNSTON.

TELEGRAM.

Richmond, July 11, 1863.

To General Joseph E. Johnston, Jackson, Miss.:

Dispatch of this day received, and remarks on defects of entrenched line noted. Though late to attempt improvement, every effort should be made to strengthen the line of defence, and compel the enemy to assault. Am deeply distressed at report of desertions. Cannot the

Governor aid you to check them by employing citizens as guards at the fords?

Beauregard and Bragg are both threatened—the former now engaged with enemy. We are entitled to discharge of the paroled prisoners, and the War Department will spare no effort to promptly secure it.

The importance of your position is apparent, and you will not fail to employ all available means to ensure success.

I have too little knowledge of your circumstances to be more definite, and have exhausted my power to aid you.

(Signed,)   JEFFERSON DAVIS.

TELEGRAM.

JACKSON, July 12, 1863.

To his Excellency, President DAVIS:

Your dispatch of 11th received. A heavy cannonade this morning for two hours from batteries east of the Canton and south of the Clinton road. The enemy's rifles (?) reached all parts of the town, showing the weakness of the position and untenableness (?) against a powerful artillery.

Breckinridge's front, south of the town, was assaulted this morning, but not vigorously. A party of skirmishers of the first, third, fourth Florida, forty-seventh Georgia and Cobb's battery took the enemy's flank and captured two hundred (200) prisoners, and colors of the twenth-eighth, forty first and fifty-third Illinois regiments. Heavy skirmishing all day yesterday.

(Signed,)   J. E. JOHNSTON.

TELEGRAPH IN CYPHER.

JACKSON, July 12, 1863.

To his Excellency, President DAVIS:

I have just learned from Colonel Logan that Port Hudson capitulated, at 6 A. M., on the 9th instant. Terms not given.

(Signed,)   J. E. JOHNSTON.

Received in Richmond, July 13, 1863.

TELEGRAM.

Richmond, Va., July 13, 1863.

To General Joseph E. Johnston, *Jackson, Miss.:*

Nothing from you since Saturday. What is the state of affairs!
(Signed,) JEFFERSON DAVIS.

TELEGRAM IN CYPHER.

Jackson, July 13, 1863.

To his Excellency, the President:

Your dispatch of the 11th received. The Governor cannot help us. Under our joint call, but one hundred and seventy-six men have been obtained. I think Grant will keep the Vicksburg prisoners until operations here are ended. He may be strongly reinforced from Port Hudson. If the position and works were not bad, want of stores which could not be collected, would make it impossible to stand siege. If the enemy will not attack we must; or, at the last moment, withdraw. We cannot attack seriously without risking the army; but it is diffiult to yield this vital point without a struggle. On afternoon of 11th, the enemy extended his right to Pearl river.
(Signed,) J. E. JOHNSTON.

Received in Richmond, July 13, 1863.

TELEGRAM.

Jackson, July 13, 1863.

To his Excellency, the President:

Colonel Fuller has just arrived from Vicksburg. The Federals issued (31,000) thirty-one thousand rations to the garrison after the siege. There were (18,000) eighteen thousand men fit for duty in the trenches the day of the surrender; about (6,000) six thousand sick and wounded in hospitals.

Loses, killed and wounded, during the siege, supposed to be twenty-five hundred (2500). General Green the only general officer killed. The garrison left Vicksburg on the 11th, and will reach a point ten miles east of Brandon, on Wednesday the 15th. Colonel Fuller thinks the troops are much demoralized, and a large proportion of the men will straggle; the cause is their objection to going to a paroled camp.

They ask a furlough of thirty days, which General Pemberton recommends. Subsisting these men will be attended with serious difficulty.
(Signed,) J. E. JOHNSTON.

TELEGRAM.

RICHMOND, VA., July 14, 1863.

To General JOSEPH E. JOHNSTON, *Jackson, Mississippi:*

Your dispatch of yesterday, received. If lists of paroled prisoners, as heretofore directed, be promptly furnished, there will be no need to detain the men in a paroled camp, as we shall insist on immediate discharge, and give to them an opportunity again to serve their country.
(Signed,) JEFFERSON DAVIS.

TELEGRAM IN CYPHER.

JACKSON, MISS., July 14, 1863.

To his Excellency, **President** DAVIS:

We learn from Vicksburg, that a large force lately left that place to turn us on the north. This will compel us to abandon Jackson. The troops before us have been entrenching and erecting batteries since their arrival.
(Signed,) J. E. JOHNSTON.

Received at Richmond, July 15th, 1863.

RICHMOND, July 15, 1863.

To General JOSEPH E. JOHNSTON:

GENERAL: Your dispatch of the 5th instant, stating that you "considered" your "assignment to the immediate command in Mississippi," as giving you a "new position," and as "limiting your authority," being a "repetition of a statement which you were informed was a grave error, and being persisted in after your failure to point out, when requested, the letter or dispatch justifying you in such a conclusion, rendered it necessary, as you were informed in my dispatch of the 8th instant, that I should make a more extended reply than could be given in a telegram That there may be no possible room for further mistake in this matter, I am compelled to recapitulate the substance of all orders and instructions given to you, so far as they bear on this question.

On the 24th November, last, you were assigned, by special order, No. 275, to a defined geographical command. The description included a portion of western North Carolina and northern Georgia, the States of Tennessee, Alabama and Mississippi, and that portion of the State of Louisiana, east of the Mississippi river. The order concluded in the following language:

"General Johnston will for the purpose "of correspondence and reports, establish his headquarters at Chattanooga, or such other place as in his judgment, will best secure communication with the troops within the limits of his command, and will repair in person to any part of said command, wherever his presence may for the time be necessary or desirable."

This command, by its terms, embraced the armies under command of General Bragg, in Tennessee, of General Pemberton, at Vicksburg, as well as those at Port Hudson, Mobile and the forces in east Tennessee.

This general order has never been changed nor modified, so as to effect your command in a single particular, nor has your control over it been interfered with. I have, as commander-in-chief, given you some orders, which will be hereafter noticed, not one of them, however, indicating in any manner that the general control confided to you, was restricted or impaired.

You exercise this command, by visiting in person, the armies at Murfreesboro,' Vicksburg, Mobile and elsewhere; and on the 22d January, I wrote to you directing that you should repair in person to the army at Tullahoma, on account of a reported want of harmony and confidence between General Bragg and his officers and troops; this letter closed with the following passage: "As that army is part of your command, no order will be necessary to give you authority there, as whether present or absent, you have a right to direct its operations, and to do whatever belongs to the general commanding."

Language cannot be plainer than this, and although the different armies in your geographical district, were ordered to report directly to Richmond as well as to yourself; this was done solely to avoid the evil that would result from reporting through you, when your headquarters might be, and it was expected frequently would be, so located as to create delays injurious to the public interest.

While at Tullahoma, you did not hesitate to order troops from General Pemberton's army, and learning that you had ordered the division of cavalry from north Mississippi to Tennessee, I telegraphed to you that this order left Mississippi exposed to cavalry raids, without means of checking them. You did not change your orders, and although I thought them injudicious, I refrained from exercising my authority in defference to your views.

When I learned that prejudice and malignity had so undermined the confidence of the troops at Vicksburg in their commander, as to threaten disaster, I deemed the circumstances such as to present the case foreseen in special order No. 275, that you should "repair, in person, to any part of said command, whenever your presence might be, for the time, necessary or desirable."

You were, therefore, ordered, on the 9th May, to "proceed at once to Mississippi, and take chief command of the forces, giving to those in the field, as far as practicable, the encouragement and benefit of your personal direction."

Some details were added about reinforcements, but not a word affecting, in the remotest degree, your authority to command your geographical district.

On the 4th June, you telegraphed to the Secretary of War in response to his inquiry, saying "my only plan is to relieve Vicksburg. My force is far too small for the purpose. Tell me if you can increase it, and how much." To which he answered, on the 5th, " I regret inability to promise more troops, as we have drained resources even to the danger of several points. You know best concerning Gen. Bragg's army; but I fear to withdraw more. We are too far outnumbered in Virginia to spare any," &c., &c.

On the 8th June, the Secretary was more explicit, if possible. He said: "Do you advise more reinforcements from Gen. Bragg? You, as commandant of the department, have power so to order if you, in view of the whole case, so determine."

On the 10th June, you answered that it was for the Government to determine what department could furnish the reinforcements; that you could not know how General Bragg's wants compared with yours; and that the Government could make the comparison. Your statements, that the Government in Richmond was better able to judge of the relative necessities of the armies under your command, than you were, and the further statement, that you could not know how Gen. Bragg's wants compared with yours, were considered extraordinary; but, as they were accompanied by the remark that the Secretary's dispatch had been imperfectly deciphered, no observation was made on them till the receipt of your telegram to the Secretary of the 12th instant, stating "I have not considered myself commanding in Tennessee since assignment here, and should not have felt authorized to take troops from that department, after having been informed by the Executive that no more could be spared."

My susprise at these two statements was extreme. You had never been "assigned" to the Mississippi command. You went there under the circumstances and orders already quoted, and no justification whatever is percived for your abandonment of your duties as commanding general of the geographical district to which you were assigned.

Orders as explicit as those under which you were sent to the west, and under which you continued to act up to the 9th May, when you were directed to repair, in person, to Mississippi, can only be impaired or set aside by subsequent orders equally explicit ; and your announcement that you had ceased to consider yourself charged with the control of affairs in Tennessee, because ordered to repair in person to Missiesippi both places being within the command to which you were assigned, was too grave to be overlooked; and when to this was added the assertion that you should not have felt authorized to draw troops from that department (Tennesse,) "after being informed by the Executive that no more could be spared," I was unable to account for your language, being entirely confident that I had never given you any such information.

I shall now proceed to separate your two statements, and begin with that which relates to your "not considering" yourself commanding in Tennessee, since assignment "here," i. e., in Mississippi.

When you received my telegram of the 15th June, informing you that "the orders to go to Mississippi did not diminish your authority in Tennessee, both being in the country placed under your command in original assignment," accompanied by an enquiry about the information, said to have been derived from me, restricting your authority to transfer troops, your answer on the 16th June, was, "I meant to tell the Secretary of War that I considered the order directing me to command here, as limiting my authority to this department, especially when that order was accompanied by War Department orders transferring troops from Tennessee to Mississippi."

This is, in substance, a repetition of the previous statement, without any reason being given for it. The fact of orders being sent to you to transfer some of the troops in your department from one point to another to which you were proceeding in person, could give no possible ground for your "considering" that special order No. 275, was recinded or modified.

Your command of your geographical district did not make you independent of my orders as your superior officer, and when you were directed by me to take troops with you to Mississippi, your control over the district to which you were assigned was in no way involved. But the statement that troops were transferred from Tennessee to Mississippi, by orders of the War Department, when you were directed to repair to the latter State, gives but half the fact; for, although you were ordered to take with you three thousand good troops, you were told to replace them by a greater number, then on their way to Mississippi, and whom you were requested to divert to Tennessee. The purpose being to hasten reinforcements to Pemberton, without weakening Bragg. This was in deference to your own opinion that Bragg could not be safely weakened—nay, that he ought even to be reinforced at Pemberton's expense, for you had just ordered troops from Pemberton's command to reinforce Bragg. I differed in opinion from you, and thought Vicksburg far more exposed to danger than Bragg, and was urging forward reinforcements to that point both from Carolina and Virginia, before you were directed to assume command in person in Mississippi.

I find nothing then, either in you dispatch of the 16th June, nor in any subsequent communication from you, giving a justification for your saying that you "had not considered yourself commanding in

Tennessee since assignment here," (*i. e.*, in Mississippi.) Your dispatch of the 5th instant, is again a substantial repetition of the same statement, without a word of reason to justify it. You say, "I considered my assignment to the immediate command in Mississippi as giving me a new position, and limiting my authority to this department." I have characterised this as a grave error, and, in view of all the facts, cannot otherwise regard it. I must add that a review of your correspondence shows a constant desire on your part, beginning early in January, that I should change the order, placing Tennessee and Mississippi in one command, under your direction, and a constant indication, on my part, whenever I wrote on the subject, that, in my judgement, the public service required that the two armies should be subject to your control.

I now proceed to your second statement in your telegram of the 12th June*, that "you should not have felt authorized to take troops from that department, (Tennessee,) after having been informed by the Executive that no more could be spared."

To my inquiry for the basis of this statement, you answered, on the 16th, by what was, in substance, a reiteration of it.

I again requested on the 17th, that you should refer by date to any such communication as that alleged by you.

You answered on the 20th June, apologized for carelessness in your first reply, and referred me to a passage from my telegram to you of the 28th May, and to one from the Secretary of War of 5th June, and then informed me that you considered "Executive" as including Secretary of War.

Your telegram of 12th June, was addressed to the Secretary of War, in the second person; it begins, "your dispatch," and then speaks of the Executive in the third person, and, on reading it, it was not supposed that the word "Executive" referred to any one but myself; but, of course, in a matter like this, your own explanation of your meaning is conclusive.

The telegram of the Secretary of War, of 5th June, followed by that of 8th of June, conveyed unmistakably, the very reverse of the meaning you attributed to them, and your reference to them as supporting your position is unintelligible. I revert, therefore, to my telegram of 28th May. That telegram was in answer to one from you in which you stated that on the arrival of certain reinforcements, then on the way, you would have about twenty-three thousand. That Pemberton could be saved only by beating Grant; and, you added: "Unless you can promise more troops we must try with that number. The odds against us will be very great. Can you add seven thousand?"

My reply was "the reinforcements sent to you exceed by, say, seven thousand, the estimate of your dispatch of 27th instant. We have withheld nothing which it was practicable to give you. We cannot hope for numerical equality, and time will probably increase the disparity."

It is on this language that you rely to support a statement that I

---

*To Secretary of War.

informed you no more troops could be spared from Tennessee, and as restricting your right to withdraw troops from that department. It bears no such construction. The reinforcements sent to you, with an exception presently to be noticed, were from points outside of your department. You had, in telegrams of 1st, 2d* and 7th May, and others, made repeated applications to have troops withdrawn from other departments to your aid. You were informed that we would give all the aid we possibly could. Of your right to order any change made in the distribution of troops in your own district, no doubt had ever been suggested by yourself nor could occur to your superiors here, for they had given you the authority.

The reinforcements which went with you from Tennessee were (as already explained, and, as was communicated to you at the time,) a mere exchange for other troops sent from Virginia.

The troops subsequently sent to you from Bragg were forwarded by him under the following dispatch from me, of 22d May: "The vital issue of holding the Mississippi at Vicksburg, is dependent on the success of General Johnston in an attack on the investing force. The intelligence from there is discouraging. Can you aid him?" If so. *and you are without orders from General Johnston*, act on your judgment."

The words that I now underscore suffice to show how thoroughly your right of command of the troops in Tennessee was recognized. I know from your own orders that you thought it more advisable to draw troops from Mississippi to reinforce Bragg than to send troops from the latter to Pemberton; and one of the reasons which induced the instruction to you to proceed to Mississippi, was the conviction that your views on this point would be changed on arrival in Mississippi. Still, although convinced myself that troops might be spared from Bragg's army without very great danger, and that Vicksburg was, on the contrary, in immediate peril, I was unwilling to overrule your judgment of the distribution of your troops while you were on the spot, and, therefore, simply left to General Bragg the power to aid you, if he could, *and if you had not given contrary orders.*

The cavalry sent to you from Tennessee was sent on a similar dispatch from the Secretary of War to General Bragg, informing him of your earnest appeal for cavalry, *and asking him if he could spare any*. Your request was for a regiment of cavalry to be sent to you from Georgia. My dispatch of 18th of May, pointed out to you the delay which a compliance would involve, and suggested that cavalry could be drawn from "another part of your department," as had been previously indicated.

In no manner, by no act, by no language, either of myself or of the Secretary of War, has your authority to draw troops from one portion of your department to another been withdrawn, restricted or modified.

Now that Vicksburg has disastrously fallen, this subject would present no pressing demand for attention, and its examination would have been postponed to a future period, had not your dispatch of the

---
*Dated May 1, received May 2, 1863.

5th instant, with its persistent repetition of statements which I had informed you were erroneous, and without adducing a single fact to sustain them, induced me to terminate the matter at once by a review of all the facts. The original mistakes in your telegram of the 12th June, would gladly have been overlooked as accidental, if acknowledged when pointed out.

The perseverance with which they have been insisted on, has not permitted me to pass them by as a mere oversight, or by refraining from an answer to seem to admit the justice of the statement.

Respectfully, &c.,
(Signed,)   JEFFERSON DAVIS.

TELEGRAM IN CYPHER.

JACKSON, July 15, 1863.

To President DAVIS:

The enemy will not attack, but has entrenched. Is evidently making a siege which we cannot resist. It would be madness to attack him. In the beginning it might have been done; but I thought then that want of water would compel him to attack us. It is reported by some of its officers, who were here yesterday, and by some gentlemen of Brandon, that the Vicksburg garrison is diminishing rapidly. Incessant but slight cannonading kept up. Our loss in killed and wounded about three hundred and fifty, (350.) The remainder of the army under Grant, at Vicksburg, is, beyond doubt, on its way to this place.

(Signed,)   J. E. JOHNSTON.

TELEGRAM IN CYPHER.

JACKSON, July 16, 1863.

To His Excellency, President DAVIS:

The enemy being strongly reinforced and able, when he pleases, to cut us off, I shall abandon this place, which it is impossible for us to hold.

(Signed,)   J. E. JOHNSTON.

TELEGRAM.

JACKSON, July 16, 1863.

To His Excellency, President DAVIS:

Your dispatch of yesterday* received. Lieutenant General Pemberton has been instructed to send an officer to Richmond with lists of paroled prisoners. Reports indicate that few of them will re-enter the service very soon as they are rapidly dispersing. Little firing yesterday. None this morning. I sent a body of cavalry to the enemy's rear afternoon of 14th, but have not heard from it.
 (Signed,)   J. E. JOHNSTON.

TELEGRAM.

BRANDON, July 17, 1863.

To his Excellency, the President:

Jackson was abandoned last night. The troops are now moving through this place to encamp three miles to the east. Those officers who have seen the Vicksburg troops, think that they cannot be kept together. General Pemberton thinks the best policy to furlough them by regiments.
 (Signed,)   J. E. JOHNSTON.

TELEGRAM IN CYPHER.

RICHMOND, VA., July 18, 1863.

To General J. E. JOHNSTON, *Brandon, Miss.:*

Your dispatch of yesterday received, informing me of your retreat from Jackson towards the east. I desire to know your ulterior purpose. The enemy may not pursue, but move up the Central road, lay waste the rich country towards Tennessee, and co-operate afterwards with Rosecranz. Another column, eastern Louisiana being abandoned, may be sent from New Orleans to attack Mobile on the land side.

The recommendation to furlough the paroled troops from Vicksburg offers a hard alternative under the pressure of our present condition.
 (Signed,)   JEFFERSON DAVIS.

---

*Dated Richmond, July 14, 1863.

TELEGRAM.

JULY 19, 1863.

To his Excellency, the President:

Your dispatch of yesterday cannot be deciphered. My purpose is to hold as much of the country as I can, and to retire further only when compelled to do so. Should the enemy cross Pearl river, I will oppose his advance; and, unless you forbid it, order General Bragg to join me to give battle. Prisoners all say that Mobile is to be attacked. I will reinforce the garrison, if necessary, not expecting Sherman to move through Mississippi at present. He must repair railroads first, and our cavalry can break them behind him. In the meantime, I will try to restore discipline.

(Signed,)   J. E. JOHNSTON.

TELEGRAM.

RICHMOND, July 21, 1863.

To General J. E. JOHNSTON, *near Morton, Miss.:*

Return to me the cypher dispatch of 18th to enable me to learn why my cypher dispatches to you are illegible.

(Signed,)   JEFFERSON DAVIS.

CAMP NEAR MORTON, July 22, 1863.

To his Excellency, the President:

As it is of the highest importance that you should have the best intelligence of the condition of military affairs in Mississippi, I have desired Brigadier General Featherstone to go to Richmond to give you information which he, an eminent Mississippian and distinguished soldier, can communicate better than any other officer of this army.

In selecting General Featherstone for this service, I have been influenced as much by my belief of your high opinion of him as by my own.

Most respectfully,
Your obedient servant,
J. E. JOHNSTON, *General.*

TELEGRAM.

Morton, July 23, 1863.

To his Excellency, the President:

Two divisions of the enemy drove our cavalry through Brandon, and returned to Jackson next day. Scouts report railroad bridges destroyed by them. Prisoners say that they will attack Mobile next. A paroled prisoner reports to Colonel Wirt Adams that a garrison of one corps was left in Jackson, the rest going to Vicksburg. Large quantities of artillery ammunition are being sent from Vicksburg. Said in the army that they are to move *via* Memphis and Mobile and Ohio road.

Desertions continue, especially of Mississippians. I shall visit Mobile in a day or two, Lieutenent General Hardee being here.

(Signed,)   J. E. JOHNSTON.

TELEGRAM IN CYPHER.

Near Morton, July 24, 1863.

To his Excellency, the President:

Brigadier General Cosby reports that the enemy's rear-guard left Jackson yesterday towards Vicksburg, and that Colonel Tom Taylor met General Sherman at Edward's depot and was told by him that his troops would not stay a day in Vicksburg, but instantly move up the river.

Does this indicate reinforcing Meade? A deserter said yesterday that these troops expect to go to Richmond.

(Signed,)   J. E. JOHNSTON.

CORRESPONDENCE

BETWEEN THE

WAR DEPARTMENT, ADJ'T & INSPECTOR GENERAL,

AND

GENERAL J. E. JOHNSTON.

C. S. A., War Department,
Richmond, Va. January 8, 1863.

To the President of the Confederate States:

Sir: I have the honor to transmit copies of "the orders given to, and correspondence with, General Joseph E. Johnston, during the months of May, June and July, 1863, concerning his command, and the operations in his department," by this Department, as called for by a resolution of the House of Representatives, adopted on the 11th December last.

Copies of the order assigning General Johnston to command, and of those constituting General Bragg's a separate department, with the accompanying correspondence, are also sent, in further elucidation of the subject.

Respectfully, your obedient servant,
JAMES A. SEDDON,
Secretary of War.

[*Extract.*]   Adjutant and Inspector General's Office,
Richmond, November 24, 1862.

SPECIAL ORDERS,
No. 275.

* * * * * * *

III. General J. E. Johnston, C. S. A., is hereby assigned to the following geographical command, to-wit: Commencing with the Blue Ridge range of mountains running through the western part of North Carolina, and following the line of said mountains through the northern part of Georgia to the railroad south from Chattanooga; thence by that road to West Point, and down the west or right bank of the Chattahoochie river, to the boundary of Alabama and Florida; following that boundary west to the Choctahatchie river, and down that river to Choctahatchie bay, (including the waters of that bay,) to the Gulf of Mexico. All that portion of country west of said line to the Mississippi river, is included in the above command. General Johnston will, for the purpose of correspondence and reports, establish his headquarters at Chattanooga, or such other place as, in his judgment, will best secure facilities for ready communication with the troops within the limits of his command, and will repair, in person, to any part of said command whenever his presence may for the time be necessary or desirable.

*   *   *   *   *   *   *

By command of the Secretary of War.

JOHN WITHERS,
Assistant Adjutant General.

TULLAHOMA, May 1, 1863.

General S. COOPER, *Adjutant and Inspector General:*

General Pemberton reports from Vicksburg to-day a furious battle has been going on since daylight. General Bowen, commanding, says he is outnumbered terribly. He has about eight thousand. Enemy's army can cross Bruinsburg, below Bayou Pierre. Lieutenant Colonel Barteau at Attolona, telegraphs to him three thousand (3,000) enemy crossed Tallahatchie at New Albany yesterday. General Pemberton calls for heavy reinforcements. They cannot be sent without giving up Tennessee; can one or two brigades be sent from the east.

(Signed,)   J. E. JOHNSTON, *General.*

TULLAHOMA, TENN., May 1, 1863.

General S. COOPER:

Reports of our scouts in Kentucky indicate invasion of east Tennessee by a strong force under Burnside. Cannot our troops there be reinforced from western Virginia or elsewhere.

(Signed,)   J. E. JOHNSTON, *General.*
(Official,)
JOHN WITHERS, *Lt. Col. and A. A. G.*

Respectfully submitted to the Secretary of War.

ENDORSED, VIZ:

Adjutant General: Telegraph this to General Sam Jones. Add, that if in his power to render the aid he will do so. He must exercise his judgment in view of the circumstances of the situation and his own forces.

May 2, 1863.

J. A. S.,
Secretary of War.

Tullahoma, Tenn., May 7, 1863.

To General S. Cooper:

Both General Pemberton and General Maury ask for reinforcements, and need them greatly. It is reported that General Foster's troops have left South Carolina. Cannot General Beauregard and Major General Jones spare troops to reinforce Mississippi and east Tennessee.

    (Signed,)   J. E. JOHNSTON, *General.*

Tullahoma, May 7, 1863.

To General S. Cooper:

I have just received the painful intelligence of the death of the distinguished Major General Van Dorn, which occurred this morning at Spring Hill.

    (Signed,)   J. E. JOHNSTON.

Tullahoma, Tenn., May 9, 1863.

General S. Cooper:

I earnestly recommend to the War Department that General Bragg's command be extended over east Tennessee. It is of great importance.

    (Signed,)   J. E. JOHNSTON, *General.*

C. S. A., War Department,
Richmond, May 9, 1863.

General J. E. Johnston, *Tullahoma, Tenn.:*

Proceed at once to Mississippi and take chief command of the forces, giving to those in the field, as far as practicable, the encouragement and benefit of your personal direction. Arrange to take, for temporary service with you, or to be followed without delay, three thousand good troops who will be substituted in General Bragg's army by a large number of prisoners returned from the Arkansas Post capture and reorganized, now on their way to General Pemberton. Stop them at the point most convenient to ~~~~~~ Bragg.

You will find reinforcements from General Beauregard to General Pemberton, and more may be expected. Acknowledge receipt.
(Signed,)   JAMES A. SEDDON,
    Secretary of War.

TULLAHOMA, May 9, 1863.

Hon. JAMES A. SEDDON:

Your dispatch of this morning received. I shall go immediately, although unfit for field service.
(Signed,)   J. E. JOHNSTON.

CONFEDERATE STATES OF AMERICA,
War Department,
Richmond, May 12, 1863.

General J. E. JOHNSTON, *Jackson, Mississsppi:*

In addition to the five thousand men originally ordered from Charleston, about four thousand more will follow. I fear more cannot be spared to you.
(Signed,)   JAMES A. SEDDON.
    Secretary of War.

JACKSON, MISS., May 13, 1863.

To JAMES A. SEDDON:

I arrived this evening finding the enemy* (in?) force between this place and General Pemberton, cutting off the communication. I am too late.
(Signed,)   J. E. JOHNSTON, *General.*

CALHOUN STATION, SEVEN MILES SOUTH OF CANTON,
May 16, 1863, 7½ A. M.

Hon. J. A. SEDDON, *Richmond:*

SIR: I reported to you by telegraph, that I learned on arriving in Jackson, on the evening of the 13th, that a Federal army had just placed itself at Clinton, on the railroad to Vicksburg, ten miles from

(*So in original.)

Jackson. The brigades of Gregg and Walker had engaged this force the day before, near Raymond, and arrived in Jackson as I did. Brigadier General Gregg estimates the force which he met, and a part of which he encountered, at twenty-five thousand.

On the following morning, it was reported that a large body of Federal troops had encamped at Raymond, the night before; and about 9 o'clock, the pickets on the roads from Clinton and Raymond, reported the enemy approaching, and about four miles distant. The opposition of our troops delayed the enemy sufficiently to enable the baggage to be withdrawn, and about half past one o'clock, the troops followed, encamping that night, six and a half miles from Jackson, and yesterday here, ten and a half miles further.

A dispatch from Lieutenant General Pemberton, received yesterday, informed me that he would march on the 15th, from Edwards' station to a point seven and a half miles west of Raymond.

On leaving Jackson, I was compelled to send orders to the troops coming from the east, to halt. I have given orders to provide them with field transportation, that they may join me, to unite with General Pemberton, but wagons and horses must be brought from a distance.

The force with me, is about six thousand. General Gist commanding the halted eastern troops, reported them yesterday morning, at fifteen hundred.

I have no information from General Pemberton, except of his move to Dillon with seventeen thousand men.

I learned at Jackson, that a brigade holds Port Hudson. I have no information of the enemy's force except that written above.

My object is to unite all the troops.

    Most respectfully,
      Your obedient servant,
(Signed,)   J. E. JOHNSTON,

Endorsed as follows, to wit:

"Respectfully referred to the President for information.
        J. A. SEDDON,
27th May, 1863.   *Secretary.*"

"Read and returned to the Secretary of War. Do not perceive why a junction was not attempted, which would have made our force nearly equal in number to the estimated strength of the enemy; and might have resulted in his total defeat, under circumstances which rendered retreat or reinforcement to him, scarcely practicable.
        J. D.

        CALHOUN STATION, May 17, 1863.

To General S. COOPER:

I am just moving west, to endeavour to join General Pemberton

Brigadier General Adams has reason to think that his appointment was not confirmed. I hope the apprehension is groundless—he is very valuable—please inform me.
 (Signed,)   J. E. JOHNSTON.

CAMP BETWEEN LIVINGSTON AND BROWNSVILLE, May 18, 1863.
General S. COOPER, *Richmond :*

I enclose herewith, a copy of a letter received last night from Lieutenant General Pemberton. I have just telegraphed to you the information it contains, and added that a Mr. Shelton, of this neighborhood, who says that he left General Pemberton's headquarters yesterday, wrote to me last night, that our troops had fallen back to Vicksburg. A gentleman who said that he was just from Bovina, was here at half past ten last night, and made the same statement.

I was preparing to join General Pemberton, personally, when this information came. It is now impracticable, and would be useless.

I shall endeavor, after collecting all available troops, to hold as much of the country as possible.

Besides the garrison of Port Hudson, the strength of which I do not know, there are now about eleven thousand infantry in the department, six or seven thousand more may soon be expected; therefore, that to make it possible to relieve Vicksburg, very large reinforcements will be necessary. I hope that the Government will send, without delay, all that can possibly be spared from other points.

I suppose that General Pemberton's force before the battle, including that in Vicksburg, was near twenty-eight thousand. He has provision for sixty days. If, as he says, Haines' Bluff is untenable, the enemy using navigation of the Yazoo, can soon reduce him by siege. Whatever efforts the Government may propose to make, must therefore, be carried into immediate effect.

 Most respectfully, &c.,
          J. E. JOHNSTON, *General.*

LETTER ENCLOSED IN FOREGOING.

HEADQUARTERS DEP'T. OF MISSISSIPPI AND EAST LOUISIANA,
    Bovina, Miss., May 17, 1863.
Gen. Jos. E. JOHNSTON, *Calhoun, Mississippi :*

GENERAL: I notified you, on the morning of the 14th, of the receipt of your instructions, to move and attack the enemy towards Clinton. I deemed the movement very hazardous, preferring to remain in position behind the Big Black, and near to Vicksburg. I called a council of war, composed of all the general officers who were then with my moveable army, and placing the subject before them, (includin your instructions,) in every view in which it appeared to me, asked their opinions respectively.

A majority of the officers expressed themselves favorable to the movement indicated by you. The others, including Major Generals Loring and Stevenson, preferred a movement by which this army might endeavor to cut off the enemy's supplies from the Mississippi.

My own views were expressed as unfavorable to any movement which would remove me from my base which was and is Vicksburg.

I did not see fit, however, to place my own judgments and opinions so far in opposition as to prevent the movement altogether; but, believing the only possibility of success to be in the plan proposed, by cutting off the enemy's supplies, I directed all my disposable force, (say 17,500,) towards Raymond or Dillons, encamping the night of the 15th at Mrs Ellison's, on the main Raymond and Edward's Depot road, at a fork from which I could advance either to Raymond or Dillons.

About 7, A. M., on the 16th, the enemy advanced his skirmishers at several points. Our line of battle was quickly formed, and the position a strong one. Heavy demonstrations were made on our right, left and centre. Gradually, however, the enemy developed himself in great force against our left, under Gen. Stevenson, reinforced, after some time, by Bowen's division, and subsequently by two brigades of Loring's.

The enemy was repeatedly driven back, but, constantly throwing in fresh troops from his heavy reinforcements, we were, about 5 P. M., compelled to withdraw. This was done by the ford over Baker's Creek, (at which a temporary bridge had been laid,) crossing the middle Raymond road. Our loss was heavy. We have lost eleven pieces of artillery, and although every arrangement was made to secure the retreat of our troops, General Loring's division, which was comparatively fresh, and which covered the approach to the ford, has not yet crossed the Big Black. I am unable to account for his absence, as I know of no cause sufficient to have prevented his following the divisions of Bowen and Stevenson, neither of whom lost a man on the retreat.

I am unable to give further particulars at present. I commanded in person. I am, for the present, holding the Big Black bridge, where a heavy cannonading is now going on. There are so many points by which I can be flanked that I fear I shall be compelled to withdraw. If so, the position at Snyder's Mill will also be untenable.

General Tilghman was killed yesterday. I have about sixty days rations in Vicksburg and Snyder's. I respectfully await your instructions.

Very respectfully, &c.,
J. C. PEMBERTON,
Lieutenant General Commanding.

P. S.—I regret to say that some of Stevenson's troops behaved very badly.

CAMP BETWEEN LIVINGSTON AND BROWNSVILLE,
via Jackson and Montgomery, May 18.

General S. COOPER:

Lieutenant General Pemberton was attacked by the enemy on the morning of the 5th, near Edward's Depot, and after nine hours' fighting, was compelled to fall back behind Big Black.

Mr. Shelton, of this neighborhood, wrote last night that he was just from Lieut. Gen. Pemberton's headquarters, and that the army was falling back to Vicksburg. Mr. Robinson, just from Bovina last night, made the same report

There are two months provisions in Vicksburg. It must ultimately fall, unless we can assemble an army to relieve. I can gather, in a few days, eleven thousand, besides a garrison at Port Hudson. Send us Anderson's cavalry regiment from the Isle of Hope, Georgia; we need it greatly.

(Signed,)   J. E. JOHNSTON, *General.*

C. S. A., WAR DEPARTMENT,
Richmond, May 19th, 1862.

General J. E. JOHNSTON, *Jackson, Miss.*:

The following dispatch just received from General Bragg:

"SHELBYVILLE, May 18.

"A brigade of cavalry from north Alabama moved to Mississippi several days ago. Another division is ordered to-day.

"(Signed,)   BRAXTON BRAGG."
(Signed,)   JAMES A. SEDDON.
Secretary of War.

JACKSON, Miss., May 25, 1863.

General S. COOPER:

It is important that I should know what troops to expect. Please inform me and have them urged on; they come too slowly.

(Signed,)   J. E. JOHNSTON.

RICHMOND, VA., May 25, 1863.

General Jos. E. JOHNSTON, *Jackson, Miss.*:

General Bragg telegraphs the President, the 23d, that he sent with you three thousand five hundred, three battalions of artillery and two thousand cavalry, and will dispatch six thousand more immediately. No troops have been ordered from this quarter, except about seven

thousand from General Beauregard's command, which it is presumed have already joined you.
(Signed,)   S. COOPER,
Adj't. and Inpector General.

CANTON, May 26, 1863.

To General S. COOPER :

Please remind the President that, in my dispatch of the 21st, I stated that two (2) major generals would be required in Mississippi. Let me urge immediate action. Could not Brig. Gen. Davis' brigade be sent?
(Signed,)   J. E. JOHNSTON,

LETTER.

C. S. A., WAR DEPARTMENT,
Richmond, May 27th, 1863.

General Jos. E. JOHNSTON, *commanding, &c.* :

GENERAL : Brigadier General J. G. Rains, having been detailed for duty in connection with torpedoes and sub-terra shells, has been ordered to report to you.

The President has confidence in his inventions, and is desirous that they should be employed both on land and river, if opportunity offers, at Vicksburg and its vicinity. Should communications allow, you are desired to send him there ; but, if otherwise, to employ him in his devices against the enemy, where most assailable in that way, elsewhere. All reasonable facilities and aid in the supply of men or material for the fair trial of his torpedoes and shells, are requested on your part. Such means of offence against the enemy are approved and recognized by the department as legitimate weapons of warfare.

With high esteem, very truly yours,
(Signed,)   JAMES A. SEDDON,
Secretary of War.

JACKSON, May 27, 1863.

To the Hon. J. A. SEDDON, *Secretary of War, Richmond :*

SIR : Saturday night, May 9, I received, at Tullahoma, your order, by telegraphic despatch, to proceed to Mississippi and take immediate command of the army. I started the next morning.

At Lake Station I received a dispatch from Lieutenant General Pemberton, directed to Tullahoma, asking for reinforcements, as the enemy in large force was moving easterly from the Mississippi, south of the Big Black, and stating that Edward's depot, their probable destination, would be the battle-field.

I arrived in Jackson on Wednesday evening, May 13, and learned from Brigadier General Gregg, who had just arrived, that he had about 5,000 men; also that Sherman's corps, four divisions, occupied Clinton.

Immediately I dispatched written messages by couriers to Lieutenant General Pemberton, informing him of my arrival and of the occupation of Clinton by Sherman's corps, four divisions, as I had been informed. I urged the importance of re-establishing communication, that he might be reinforced; ordered that he should, if practicable, come upon the enemy's rear at once, with all the strength he could quickly assemble; informing him that we could co-operate in such an attack.

On Tuesday, May 14, after all preparation had been completed, and orders to Brigadier Generals Gist and Maxey for the security of their commands had been given, I evacuated Jackson about noon, being obliged to take the Canton road at right angles to that upon which the enemy approached.

That evening, from our camp about six miles from Jackson, I sent dispatch to Lieutenant General Pemberton, informing him that General Gregg and his command had been compelled to evacuate Jackson, and of the direction taken; that Brigadier General Gist had been ordered to assemble the approaching troops at a point forty or fifty miles from Jackson, and Brigadier General Maxey to return to his wagons, and advised to join Brigadier General Gist; expressed the hope that this force would be able to prevent the enemy in Jackson from drawing provision from the east, and that Brigadier General Gregg's force would be able to keep him from the country towards Panola; inquired if the enemy could not be cut off from his supplies from the Mississippi; and, above all, should the enemy, from want of supplies, be compelled to fall back, could he (General Pemberton) not beat him? I strongly urged concentration of troops.

On Friday morning, May 15, I received dispatch from Lieutenant General Pemberton, dated 5.40 P. M., Edward's depot, May 14, stating that he would move early next morning with a column of seventeen thousand men, to Dillons, situated on the main road leading from Raymond to Port Gibson, seven and a half miles below Raymond, and nine and a half miles from Edward's depot, to cut the enemy's communication, and force the enemy to attack him, as he did not consider his force sufficient to justify his attacking the enemy in position, or cutting his way to Jackson. This dispatch was brought by Captain Yerger, who bore the dispatch of the 13th instant to General Pemberton.

I immediately acknowledged receipt of the above dispatch, and ansered General Pemberton that our movement to the north rendered his plan of junction by Raymond impracticable, and ordered him to move so as to effect a junction, and to communicate with me so that I might unite to his force about six thousand men. The copy of this dispatch (sent from a point on the Jackson and Canton road, about ten miles from Jackson,) was mislaid, and cannot at present be found.

On Saturday, May 16, at Calhoun station, I received a dispatch from Lieutenant General Pemberton, dated 9.10, A. M., Bovina, May 14, stating that he moves at once from Edward's depot, with his whole available force; explaining disposition of his troops, and closing dispatch by stating that he at once complies with my order. This dispatch I received in the afternoon, having waited here all day to be advised by General Pemberton of the direction of his movements. In the evening of the same day I received a dispatch from General Pemberton, dated 8, A. M., four miles south of Edward's, May 16, acknowledging receipt of my letter written from the Canton road—stating that he received it at half-past six o'clock that morning; that it found the army in the middle road to Raymond; that he had issued the order of countermarch; that owing to destruction of bridge on Baker's Creek his march would be on the road from Edward's depot in the direction of Brownsville; that in going to Clinton he would leave Bolton's Depot to the right. In a postscript he reported heavy skirmishing then going on his front.

On Sunday, May 17th, I marched fifteen miles in the direction indicated in General Pemberton's note, and, on that evening, Captain Henderson brought me a letter from General Pemberton, dated Bovina, May 17th, giving me intelligence of his being compelled, on the 16th instant, after engaging the enemy, to withdraw, with heavy loss, to Big Black Bridge. A copy of this letter I forwarded that night to General Cooper.

General Pemberton expressed fears that he would be compelled to fall back from Big Black Bridge, and, if so, he represented that the position at Snyder's Mill would also be untenable.

During the night I received information that General Pemberton had fallen back to Vicksburg. I then determined, by easy marches, to establish my line between Jackson and Canton, as the junction of the two commands had become impossible. During that night, after having received the above information, I sent a dispatch to General Pemberton, that if Haynes' Bluff be untenable Vicksburg is of no value, and cannot be held. Evacuate the place, if not rendered too late by investment, to save the troops.

On Monday, the 18th instant, near Vernon, I received a letter from General Pemberton, dated Vicksburg, May 17th, informing me that he had fallen back to the line of entrenchments around Vicksburg, having been attacked and forced back from Big Black Bridge. Also, that he had ordered the abandonment of Snyder's Mill.

On the 19th instant, I received a letter from General Pemberton acknowledging the receipt of my communication in reply to his brought by Captain Henderson, and stating that he assembled a council of war of the general officers of his command, who unanimously expressed the opinion upon my instructions, that it was impossible to withdraw the army from Vicksburg with such morale and materiel as to be of further service to the Confederacy.

On the 19th instant, I sent orders, by telegraphic dispatches and by couriers, to Major General Gardner to evacuate Port Hudson.

On the 20th and 21st instant, the brigades of Generals Gist, Ector and McNair, joined my command. The last troops of Brigadier General Evans' brigade, arrived on the day before yesterday.

Major General Loring, with his command, arrived here about the 19th instant, and Brigadier General Maxcy's brigade on the 23d instant.

The troops above mentioned, with General Breckinridge's division of General Bragg's army, will make a force of about twenty-three thousand effective men. Grant's army is estimated at sixty thousand or eighty thousand men, and his troops are worth double the number of north-eastern troops. We cannot relieve General Pemberton, except by defeating Grant, who is believed to be fortifying. We must make the attempt with such a force as the Government can furnish for the object. Unless more may be expected, the attempt must be made with the force now here and that coming. If possible, however, additional troops should be sent to make up an army of at least thirty thousand men—infantry. Even that force would be small for the object.

An army of twenty-three thousand men, for offensive operations against Grant, seems to me too small, considering his large force. We need, very much, good general officers.

I find it necessary to organize an army, and to provide for it subsistence, ammunition and means of transportation.

Most respectfully, your obedient servant,
(Signed.) J. E. JOHNSTON, *General.*
"Respectfully referred to the President for his information.
"J. A. SEDDON,
"*Secretary of War.*"

JUNE 13th, 1863.

JACKSON, May 28, 1863.

To Hon. J. A. SEDDON, *Secretary of War:*

I respectfully ask that surgeon D. W. Yandell, Medical Director, Hardee's corps, be assigned as medical director of my command. He is now on duty with me. Be pleased to answer by telegraph.
(Signed,) J. E. JOHNSTON, *General.*

CONFEDERATE STATES OF AMERICA, WAR DEPARTMENT,
Richmond, May 30, 1863.

General Jos. E. JOHNSTON, *Jackson, Miss.:*

Surgeon D. W. Yandell will be assigned as you desire.
(Signed, J. A. SEDDON, *Secretary of War.*

JACKSON, June 2, 1863

Hon. J. A. SEDDON, *Secretary of War:*

Your letter of the 25th, and a telegram from the President, show that you are misinformed as to the force at my disposal. The effective force, infantry and artillery, is, from Lieutenant General Pemberton, *nine thousand eight hundred and thirty-one;** from General Bragg, *seven thousand nine hundred and thirty-nine;* from General Beauregard, *six thousand two hundred and eighty-three.* Total, *twenty-four thousand and fifty-three,* (24,053.)

Brigadier General Jackson's cavalry not arrived, and irregular troops protecting northern and southern frontiers not included. Grant is receiving continual accession. Tell me if it is your intention to make up the number you gave the President as my force, or if I may expect more troops. With the present force we cannot succeed without great blunders by the enemy. Each portion of this dispatch in cypher is independent of the preceding.

(Signed,)   J. E. JOHNSTON.

C. S. A., WAR DEPARTMENT,
Richmond, June 3, 1863.

To General J. E. JOHNSTON, *Jackson:*

I am *concerned** at your telegram to the President, as *to the number* of your forces. I had reported them to him as rather *more than thirty thousand*—thus made up, *thirty five hundred taken with you, ten thousand sent from Charleston, twenty-five hundred cavalry* and *six thousand infantry from General Bragg, four thousand,* at least, *under Gregg at Jackson,* on your arrival, *six thousand under Loring.* In addition, I suggested, you might have *a brigade or so from Port Hudson.* Where was the mistake on my part?

I feel intense anxiety as to your plans, and should be gratified to learn them as far as you deem safe to inform.

(Signed,)   JAMES A. SEDDON,
Secretary of War.

LITERAL COPY OF DISPATCH RECEIVED.

CANTON, June 4, 1863.

Hon. J. A. SEDDON, *Secretary of War:*

Your dispatch of yesterday, received. By mistake, on your part,

---

*Words in *italic* in cypher.

is that all your numbers are too large, in reference to Beauregard, nearly as ten (10) to six (6.) The troops you mention including Jackson's, just arrived are less than *fifty-six hundred.** My only plan is to *relieve Vicksburg, my force is far too small* for the purpose, tell me *if you can increase it* and how much. Grant is receiving reinforcements. Port Hudson is closely invested. The great object of the enemy for this campaign, is to acquire possession of the Mississippi. Can you collect here a force sufficient to defeat the object.

(Signed,) J. E. JOHNSTON.

LETTER.

CANTON, June 5, 1863.

Hon. J. A. SEDDON:

DEAR SIR: I thank you cordially for your kind letter of May 25th; but almost regret that you feel such confidence in me as is expressed in it. From the present condition of affairs, I fear that confidence dooms you to disappointment. Every day gives some new intelligence of the enemy's strength—of reinforcements on the way to him. My first intention, on learning that Lieutenant General Pemberton was in Vicksburg, was to form an army to succor him. I suppose, from my telegraphic correspondence with the Government, that all the troops to be hoped for have arrived. Our resources seem so small and those of the enemy so great, that the relief of Vicksburg is beginning to appear impossible to me. Pemberton will undoubtedly make a gallant and obstinate defence, and hold out as long as he can make resistance; but unless we assemble a force strong enough to break Grant's line of investment, the surrender of the place will be a mere question of time. General Grant is receiving reinforcements almost daily. His force, according to the best information to be had, is more than treble that which I command. Our scouts say, too, that he has constructed lines of circumvallation and has blocked up all roads leading to his position.

The enterprize of forcing the enemy's lines would be a difficult one, to a force double that at my disposal. If you are unable to increase that force decidedly, I must try to accomplish something in aid of the besieged garrison, and yet when considering it, it seems to me desperate. Yur suggestion to General Kirby Smith, was promptly dispatched to him. I have no doubt that the time is favorable for attacking Helena.

In replying by telegraph to your letter and telegrams, I have said that if you can increase this army, it should be done, if you cannot, nothing is left for us but to struggle manfully with such means as the Government can furnish.

*Words in *italic* sent in cipher

I beg you to consider, in connection with affairs in this department, that I have had not only to organize, but to provide means of transportation and supplies of all sorts for an army. The artillery is not yet equipped. All of Lieutenant General Pemberton's supplies were of course, with his troops about Vicksburg and Port Hudson. I found myself, therefore, without subsistence stores, ammunition, or the means of conveying those indispensables. It has proved more difficult to collect wagons and provisions than I expected. We have not yet the means of operating for more than four days away from the railroads—that to Vicksburg is destroyed.

We draw our provision from the northern part of the State. The protection of that country employs about twenty-five hundred irregular cavalry. It is much too small. I am endeavoring to increase it by calling for volunteers, but am by no means sanguine as to the results.

  Most respectfully,
    Your obedient servant,
(Signed,)   J. E. JOHNSTON.

RICHMOND, VA., June 5, 1863.

General J. E. JOHNSTON:

The mistake was not mine, as I rested on official reports *of numbers sent.** *I regret my inability to promise more troops,* as we have *drained resources even to the danger of several points.* You know best concerning *General Bragg's army, but I fear to withdraw more.* We are too far *outnumbered in Virginia to spare any.* You must rely on what you have and the irregular forces *Mississippi can afford.* Your judgment and skill are fully relied on, *but I venture the suggestion, that, to relieve Vicksburg, speedy action is essential.* With the facilities and resources of the enemy, time works against us.

(Signed,)   J. A. SEDDON,
           Secretary of War.

CANTON, June 5, 1863.

Hon. J. A. SEDDON:

Grant still receives reinforcements. Scouts near Friar's Point report eight boats loaded with troops passed down Monday and Tuesday. Twelve empty transports passed up.

(Signed,)   J. E. JOHNSTON.

---

*Words in *italic* in cypher.

CANTON, June 5, 1863.

Hon. J. A. SEDDON:

Brigadier General Whitfield, who was ordered to report to me when I was in Tennessee, but could not, has just done so. What is your intention in regard to him? I am informed that it will be *very unfortunate** for him to *command* the brigade to which he has belonged.
    (Signed,)   J. E. JOHNSTON.

RICHMOND, June 8, 1863.

To General J. E. JOHNSTON, *Canton, Miss.:*

General Whitfield* was believed to be peculiarly acceptable to *his* brigade. What is the objection? Do you advise *more reinforcements from General Bragg?* You, as *commandant of the department, have power so to order, if you, in view of the whole case, so determine. We cannot send from Virginia or elsewhere, for we stand already not one to two.*
    (Signed,)   J. A. SEDDON,
                                            Secretary of War.

JUNE 8, 1863.

General S. COOPER:

The following is just received from Captain Thomas Henderson, of scout service: "Panola, Miss., June 6, 1863. Scout Wilson reports eleven (11) o'clock yesterday, since Sunday seventeen (17) transports with troops, gone down the river from Memphis. All came from railroad. Grant orders all forces possible sent him. Eight thousand (8,000) wounded arrived, and large arrangements made for more.
    (Signed,)   "THOMAS S. HENDERSON."
    (Signed,)   J. E. JOHNSTON.

CANTON, June 9, 1863, *via Montgomery*, 10.

Hon. JAMES A. SEDDON:

Your dispatch of yesterday in cypher was received, but cannot be read. Please repeat it.
    (Signed,)   J. E. JOHNSTON.

---

*Words in *italic* in cypher.

JACKSON, June 10, 1863.

Hon. J. A. SEDDON, *Secretary of War:*

Your dispatch of June 8th, in cypher, received. You do not give orders in regard to the recently appointed general officers. Please do it. *I have not (?) at my half the number of troops necessary.* It is for the Government to determine what department, if any, can furnish the *reinforcements required.* I cannot know here General Bragg's wants compared with mine. The Government can make such comparisons. Your dispatch is imperfectly deciphered.

    (Signed,)   J. E. JOHNSTON.

JACKSON, June 12, 1863.

Hon. J. A. SEDDON, *Secretary of War:*

Your dispatch of the eighth (8th) imperfectly deciphered and partially answered on the 10th. I have not considered myself commanding in Tennessee since assignment here, and should not have felt authorized to take troops from that department, after having been informed by the Executive that *no more could be spared.* To take from Bragg a force which would make this army fit to oppose Grant would involve *yielding Tennessee.* It is for the Government to decide *between this State and Tennessee.*

    (Signed,)   J. E. JOHNSTON.

CAMDEN, June 13, 1863.

To General S. COOPER:

Scout, at Friar's Point, on the 9th instant, reports nine transports full of infantry and artillery went down the river since Sunday. Force supposed to be about thirteen thousand (13,000.) In addition to the above, same scout reports fourteen more transports, crowded with infantry and artillery, went down the river on the 10th instant.

    (Signed,)   J. E. JOHNSTON.

JACKSON, June 15, 1863.

Hon. JAMES A. SEDDON:

Your repeated dispatch of the 8th is deciphered. I cannot advise in regard to the points from which troops can best be taken, having no means of knowing; nor is it for me to judge which it is best, yield (or hold) Mississippi or Tennessee; that is for the Government to determine. Without some great blunder of the enemy, we cannot hold both. The odds against me are much greater than those you express. I consider saving Vicksburg hopeless.

(Signed,)   J. E. JOHNSTON.

CONFEDERATE STATES OF AMERICA,
War Department,
Richmond, June 16, 1863.

General J. E. JOHNSTON:

Your telegram *grieves and alarms me.** Vicksburg must not be lost *without a desperate struggle*. The interest and honor of the Confederacy forbid it. I rely on you still to avert *the loss*. If *better resources* do not *offer, you must hazard attack*. It may be *made* in *concert with the garrison*, if practicable, *but otherwise without, by day or night* as you think best.

(Signed,)   JAMES A. SEDDON,
Secretary of War.

JACKSON, June 16, 1863.

Hon. JAMES A. SEDDON:

General Bragg informs me that a telegram from Louisville, of the 10th, says that part of the ninth and third corps have been sent to reinforce Grant. Will not this enable us to *invade Kentucky.** For this, General Bragg's command should *extend* over *east Tennessee*.

(Signed,)   J. E. JOHNSTON, *General.*

JACKSON, June 19, 1863.

Hon. J. A. SEDDON:

A courier has arrived here with dispatches from General Gardner, of the 10th instant. The courier reports the garrison in good spirits. General Gardner states, that he has repulsed the enemy in several severe attacks, but he is still closely invested; that he is getting *short* *of provisions and ammunition, and should be speedily relieved*.

(Signed,)   J. E. JOHNSTON.

*Words in *italic* in cypher.

JACKSON, June 19, 1863.

Hon. J. A. SEDDON:

Dispatch of the 16th received. I think that you do not appreciate the difficulties in the course you direct, nor the probabilities or consequence of *failure*. Grant's position, naturally very strong, is entrenched and protected by powerful artillery, and the roads obstructed. His reinforcements have been at least equal to *my whole force*.* The Big Black *covers him* from attack, and would cut off *our retreat if defeated*. We *cannot* combine operations with *General Pemberton* from uncertain and store† *communication*. *The defeat* of this *little army* would at once *open Mississippi and Alabama* to Grant. I will do all I can, *without hope* of doing more than aid to *extricate the garrison*.

(Signed,)   J. E. JOHNSTON.

JACKSON, June 20, 1863.

Hon. J. A. SEDDON, *Secretary of War:*

On arriving here, I informed General Kirby Smith of the condition of *Vicksburg and Port Hudson**, and requested his *aid and co-operation*, which he has given.

General Taylor with *eight thousand men is opposite* Vicksburg, and temporarily *occupies Milliken's Bend* and other points on the *river*. The presence of *this force is encouraging*. Nothing can be done *by us to relieve Port Hudson*, which is *in imminent peril*. *General Taylor* will make such *demonstrations opposite Port Hudson* as he can.

(Signed,)   J. E. JOHNSTON.

RICHMOND, June 21, 1863.

General J. E. JOHNSTON, *Jackson:*

Yours of the 19th received. *Consequences** are realized and *difficulties* are recognized *as very great, but still think, other means failing*, the course recommended should *be hazarded*. *The aim*, in my judgment, *justifies any risk and all probable consequences*.

(Signed,)   JAMES A. SEDDON,
                                           Secretary of War.

---

*Words in *italic* in cypher.
†Perhaps rare.

RICHMOND, VA., June 21, 1863.

General JOSEPH E. JOHNSTON, *Jackson:*

Only my conviction (of almost imperative necessity for action) induces the official dispatch I have just sent you. On every ground I have great deference to your superior knowledge of the position, your judgement and military genius, but I feel it right to share—if need be, to take the responsibility, and leave you free to follow the most desperate course the occasion may demand. Rely upon it, the eyes and hopes of the whole Confederacy are upon you, with the full confidence that you will act; and with the sentiment that it were better to fail, nobly daring, than, through prudence even, to be inactive, I look to attack in last resort, but rely on your resources of generalship to suggest less desperate modes of relief. I can scarce dare to suggest, but might it not be possible to strike Banks first and unite the garrison of Port Hudson with you, or to secure sufficient co-operation from General Smith, or to practically besiege Grant by operations with artillery from the swamps, now dry, on the north side of the Yazoo, below Haynes' Bluff. I rely on you for all possible to save Vicksburg.

    (Signed,)   J. A. SEDDON.

JACKSON, June 22, 1863.

Hon. J. A. SEDDON:

Positive information has just been received from General E. K. Smith that fifty-seven transports troops passed Napoleon on the 11th and 12th last, going down the Mississippi river.

    (Signed,)   J. E. JOHNSTON.

CANTON, June 22, 1863.

Hon. J. A. SEDDON, *Secretary of War:*

Your dispatch of 21st received, but cannot be deciphered. Please repeat it using (?) as few words as possible in cypher.

    (Signed,)   J. E. JOHNSTON.

JACKSON, June 23, 1863.

Hon. JAMES A. SEDDON:

General Ruggles reports that on the 20th instant, attacked the enemy, eight hundred strong, with two guns, near Rocky ford on Tallahatchie. Routed him completely; captured his baggage train, ammunition and supplies, killing about fifty. Our loss small.

  (Signed,)   J. E. JOHNSTON.

                 CANTON, June 24, 1863.

Hon. JAMES A. SEDDON:

Your two dispatches of 21st received. There has been no voluntary inaction. When I came, all military materials of the department were in Vicksburg and Port Hudson. Artillery had to be brought from the east; horses for it and all field transportation procured in an exhausted country; much from Georgia brought over wretched railroads, and provisions collected. I have not had the means of moving. We cannot contend with the enemy north of the Yazoo. He can place a large force there in a few hours—we, a small one, in ten or twelve days. We cannot *relieve Port Hudson* without *giving up Jackson*, by which we should lose Mississippi. Kirby Smith sent troops to give all possible aid to Vicksburg, but they have not been used by their commanders.

  (Signed,)   J. E. JOHNSTON, *General.*

                 RICHMOND, June 26, 1863.

General JOSEPH E JOHNSTON, *Jackson, Miss:*

I have just received reliable information, through a friend from Baltimore, that Grant telegraphed for supplies and ammunition; both failing. Train of cars laden with such was sent through Baltimore ten days ago, marked for Yazoo city, to proceed *via Cairo*, under charge of a person friendly to the South and anxious to have a chance to yield them to capture. This may possibly prove useful.

  (Signed,)   JAMES A. SEDDON,
                  Secretary of War.

                 JACKSON, June 29, 1863.

To General S. COOPER:

The following dispatch has just been received,

  (Signed,)   J. E. JOHNSTON, *General.*

"ALEXANDRIA, June 26, 1863,
"*via Natchez*, 27.

"General J. E. JOHNSTON:

"I have the honor to inform you that, on the 23rd instant, General Taylor stormed, at the point of the bayonet, with unloaded muskets, the enemy's position at Berwick's Bay, capturing over one thousand (1,000) prisoners, ten heavy guns, and a large amount of stores of all descriptions—the position of Thibodeaux was also carried. This gives him command of the Mississippi river above New Orleans, and will enable him, in a great measure, to cut off Banks' supplies.

"(Signed,) E. SORGET,
"*Assistant Adjutant General.*"

TELEGRAM.

JACKSON, July 7, 1863.

Hon. J. A. SEDDON:

Vicksburg capitulated on the 4th instant. Garrison was paroled, and are to be returned, the officers retaining their side arms and personal baggage. This intelligence was brought by an officer who left the place on Sunday the 5th. In consequence, I am falling back from the Big Black river to Jackson.

(Signed,) J. E. JOHNSTON, *General.*

RICHMOND, July 7, 1863.

To General JOSEPH E. JOHNSTON, *Jackson,*

A telegram of the 5th instant, signed "Woodson," approved by T. B. Lamar, chief of staff, informing of the fall of Vicksburg, is just received. Telegraph if this be true, and any particulars known.

(Signed,) JAMES A. SEDDON,
Secretary of War.

JACKSON, July 8, 1863.

Hon. J. A. SEDDON:

Your dispatch of the seventh (7th) received. The following was sent you yesterday directly after the intelligence of the fall of Vicksburg was received: "Vicksburg capitulated on the fourth (4th) instant. The garrison was paroled, and are to be returned to our lines, the officers retaining their side arms and personal baggage. This intelligence was brought by an officer who left the place on Sunday, the fifth (5th) instant. In consequence, I am falling back from the Big Black to Jackson.

 (Signed,)   " J. E. JOHNSTON."

Colonel Montgomery has just arrived from Vicksburg. He was directed by General Pemberton to have supplies prepared at this place for twenty two thousand men, the paroled garrison of Vicksburg.

 (Signed,)   J. E. JOHNSTON.

JACKSON, July 8, 1863.

To General S. COOPER:

The paroled garrison of Vicksburg will be here in a few days. What shall be done with the men? They cannot remain in this department without great injury to us from deficiency of supplying them. Shall they go to their homes until exchanged, or be distributed in regiments in their respective States? Can they be exchanged immediately for prisoners taken in the recent great Confederate victory?

 (Signed,)   J. E. JOHNSTON.

RICHMOND, July 8, 1863.

To General J. E. JOHNSTON, *Jackson, Miss.:*

Inform fully as you know of the terms of capitulation of Vicksburg, especially the position of officers and men, in relation to parole and power of exchange.

 (Signed,)   J. A. SEDDON,
                Secretary of War.

JACKSON, July 9, 1863.

Hon. J. A. SEDDON:

I have nothing official of capitulation of Vicksburg. An officer of the garrison told me that the terms were those I stated; the troops to be paroled and sent into our lines as soon as form is complied; officers to retain baggage and side arms; soldiers their clothing. Provisions being exhausted, the general officers proposed capitulation to General Pemberton. I have not heard of the garrison.

 (Signed,)   J. E. JOHNSTON, *General.*

JACKSON, MISS., July 9, 1863.

To the President:

The enemy is advancing in two columns on Jackson, now about four miles distant. I shall endeavor to hold the place, as the possession of Mississippi depends on it. His force is about double ours.
 (Signed,)   J. E. JOHNSTON.

CONFEDERATE STATES OF AMERICA,
Executive Department,
Richmond, July 10th, 1863.

Hon. Secretary of War:

The following telegram was received by President, and is forwarded to you for your information
    Most respectfully,
     Your obedient servant,
 (Signed,)   WM. PRESTON JOHNSTON,
          Colonel and A. D. C.

BY TELEGRAPH FROM JACKSON, MISS.

" *To his Excellency, the President:*

" Your dispatch of yesterday received. No report of Taylor's junction has reached me, as it must have done if true, as we have 1,200 cavalry in that vicinity. I hear nothing official from Vicksburg.

" Major Jacob Thompson, of General Pemberton's staff, gives me the following list: Lieutenant General Pemberton, Major Generals Stevenson, Forney, M. L. Smith and Bowen; Brigadier Generals Barton, Lee, Cumming, Moore, Baldwin, Hebert, Vaughn, Shoup; Colonels Reynolds, Waul and Cockerill, commanders brigades; also Brigadier General Harris, of Missouri militia.
 (Signed,)   " J. E. JOHNSTON."

Endorsed:

" Referred to Col. Ould for information as to general officers for exchange.
               " J. A. S., *Sec.*"

July 11th, 1863.

C. S. A., WAR DEPARTMENT,
Richmond, July 10, 1863.

General J. E. JOHNSTON, *Jackson, Miss.:*

To afford facilities for exchange, at the earliest period, telegraph as soon as you know the number of privates, sergeants, corporals, lieutenants, captains, majors, lieutenant colonels, colonels, brigadiers, and generals, designating, as far as practicable, the number of the foregoing belonging to each regiment; at any rate, send the designation of the regiments captured. After full lists are prepared, you will send them on without delay, but telegraph only as above.

(Signed,)   J. A. SEDDON,
Secretary of War.

JACKSON, July 14, 1863.

To General S. COOPER:

General Pemberton has recommended that his troops be furloughed. Should the recommendation be adopted, it will have an injurious effect upon this army, unless the paroled troops are first moved to a distance. I suppose that they should move to the camp at Demopolis, and have so informed General Pemberton.

(Signed,)   J. E. JOHNSTON.

C. S. A., WAR DEPARTMENT,
Richmond, July 16, 1864.

To Gen. J. E. JOHNSTON, *Jackson, Miss.:*

The following officers, having been duly exchanged, are released from parole, and at liberty to return to service: Lieutenant General J. C. Pemberton, Major Generals Stevenson, Forney, M. L. Smith, and Bowen; Brigadier Generals Barton, Lee, Cumming, Moore, Hebert, Baldwin, Vaughan, and Shoup; Colonels Reynolds, Waul, and Cockerill, commanding brigades; also, Brigadier General Harris, Missouri militia.

(Signed,)   JAMES A. SEDDON,
Secretary of War.

C. S A., WAR DEPARTMENT, A. & I. GEN'S OFFICE,
Richmond, Va., July 22, 1863.

General JOHNSTON, *Morton, Miss.:*

In conformity with your expressed wish, you are relieved from the further command of the department of Tennessee, which, as advised by you, is united to that of East Tennessee, so as to extend General Bragg's command over the department of General Buckner.

(Signed,)   S. COOPER,
A. & I. General.

LETTER.

C. S. A., War Department,
Richmond, Va., July 24, 1863.

General Joseph E. Johnston, *commanding, &c.:*

General: The President of the Mississippi Central Railroad telegraphs that you have ordered the destruction by fire of railroad equipments, to the value of five millions dollars. The President directs that efforts be made to bring away the equipments, which should be taken down the road, for removal, as far as may be necessary.

Your obedient servant,
(Signed,)   JAMES A. SEDDON,
Secretary of War.

LETTER.

C. S. A., War Department,
Richmond, July 21, 1863.

General J. E. Johnston, *commanding, &c.:*

General: If you have not had occasion to use the funds transmitted through Commodore Barron, you will please return them by the first safe opportunity, as the Secretary of the Navy, from whose appropriations they were drawn, needs the amount for sterling exchange.

With high regard, your obedient servant,
(Signed,)   JAMES A. SEDDON,
Secretary of War.

Morton, July 24, 1863.

General S. Cooper:

Your dispatch of 22d, relieving me from command of department of Tennessee, received. Major General Maury thinks attack on Mobile threatening. I request that Clayton's brigade, belonging to Mobile garrison, and sent by me to General Bragg in emergency, may be ordered back immediately. Major General Maury has but twenty-five hundred men for land defence.

(Signed,)   J. E. JOHNSTON.

Morton, July 24, 1863.

His Excellency, the President:

Brigadier General Cosby reports that the enemy's rear guard left

Jackson yesterday, towards Vicksburg, and that Colonel Tom Taylor met General Sherman at Edward's Depot, and was told by him that his troops would not stay a day in Vicksburg, but instantly move up the river. Does this indicate reinforcing Meade? A deserter said yesterday that these troops expect to go to Richmond.

(Signed,)   J. E. JOHNSTON.

The above dispatch was in cypher.

C. S. A., WAR DEPARTMENT,
Richmond, July 25, 1863.

General J. E. JOHNSTON, *Morton, Miss.*:

I am requested by the Secretary of the Treasury to instruct that all cotton belonging to the Government, liable to fall into the hands of the enemy, which cannot be removed, be destroyed.

(Signed,)   JAMES A. SEDDON,
Secretary of War.

ADJUTANT AND INSPECTOR GENERAL'S OFFICE,
Richmond, July 25, 1863.

SPECIAL ORDERS, No. 176.

Extract.

*   *   *   *   *   *

VI. The *department of East Tennessee is merged* in the *department of Tennessee*, which will be separate and independent, reporting directly to this office.

VII. The limits of the *department of Tennessee* will embrace the country now included in the department of East Tennessee, and west of the Blue Ridge mountains, in North Carolina, and a line running south to the Georgia railroad, thence along the lines of railroad, via Atlanta, to West Point, and from that place north to the Tennessee river, and down that stream to its mouth.

*   *   *   *   *   *

By command of the Secretary of War.

JNO. WITHERS,
Assistant Adjutant General.

TELEGRAM.

MOBILE, July 29, 1863.

General S. COOPER:

I came here because Major General Maury apprehends attack. His scouts at Pensacola report Admiral Farragut went north yesterday,

which indicates no attack. Officers from Vicksburg report that all troops go up the river.
  (Signed,)   J. E. JOHNSTON.

Received at Richmond, July 30, 1863,
By telegraph from Mobile, 29.

To General S. Cooper:

What is the extent of my command. I return to Morton to night.
  (Signed,)   J. E. JOHNSTON.
A. & I. G. Office, Richmond, Va., January, 1864, official copy.

Morton, July 30, 1863.

Hon. J. A. Seddon:

I conversed, this morning, with Major Matthews, of the artillery, just from Vicksburg, who says that one of Major General M. L. Smith's staff told him that Grant had sent very few troops up the river; but about the 22d had seventeen (17) transports of troops down. Others had preceded these. Reports from different sources, *all so contradictory*, that no opinion of the enemy's intentions can be formed. The officer above named, says that the Federals destroyed everything connected with cultivation of ground between Jackson and Big Black river, including growing crops.
  (Signed,)   J. E. JOHNSTON.

Richmond, July 31, 1863.

To General J. E. Johnston, *Morton, Mississippi:*

Your command embraces the country west of the line between Georgia and Alabama, and running south to the gulf, as before General Bragg's Department was formed. Its western limit is the Mississippi river, and its northern boundary the Tennessee river and Kentucky line.
  (Signed,)   S. COOPER, *A. & I. General.*
A. & I. G. Office, Richmond, January, 1864, official copy.

Morton, July 31, 1863.

Hon. J. A Seddon, *Secretary of War:*

The following telegraph (?) is forwarded for the information of the War Department:

"Mobile, July 30, 1863.

"General J. E. Johnston:

"A gentleman, who left Vicksburg on Friday, states that Grant is still in Vicksburg. Is repairing road to Jackson. Expect bridge over Big Black to be ready for transportation of cars in about thirty days There is great and increasing sickness in the army, and their expectation is that it will be sixty days before they will move to Jackson. They propose to go to Meridian, to Demopolis and to Selma, and then invest Mobile. They were actively organizing negro regiments, which they threw across into Louisiana, as fast as organized. No large force has been sent up the river Those sent were of Burnside's corps, and troops whose time had expired. McPherson in command at Vicksburg. Parks at Snyder's Bluff. Informant is person of intelligence and veracity, with peculiar opportunities of information. Another officer, just in from New Orleans with prisoners, states that Banks' force has been recently increased from Grant, and that they propose soon sending one portion of Banks' army over into Louisiana, and another twenty thousand strong to Pascagoula. Grant is collecting immense supplies of stores at Vicksburg.

"Dabney H. Maury,
"*Major General commanding.*"

(Signed,) J. E. JOHNSTON.

Morton, August 20, 1863.

S. Cooper, *A. & I. General:*

General: I thank you for your letter of the 12th, which I have just received, with copies of so much of special orders 176 and 184, as define the limits of General Bragg's command, and your telegram to me of July 31st.

These papers cannot be misunderstood. As my apology for having troubled you more than once on this subject, I respectfully enclose copies of your telegram and paragraph vii., special orders 176, as I received them orignally. One marred by the operator; the other without the important line following the name " West Point."

Most respectfully,
Your obedient servant,
J. E. JOHNSTON, *General.*

[*Extract.*] Adjutant and Inspector General's Office,
Richmond, 1863.

SPECIAL ORDERS,
No. 176.

VII. The limits of the Department of Tennessee will embrace the country now included in the Department of east Tennessee and west of Blue Ridge mountains, in North Carolina, and a line running south to the Georgia railroad, thence along the line of railroad via Atlanta to West Point and down that stream to its mouth.

By command of the Secretary of War.

(Signed,)   JOHN WITHERS,
Assistant Adjutant General.

(Official,)
BENJ. S. EWELL, *A. A. G.*

TELEGRAM.

RICHMOND, July 31, 1863.

General J. E. JOHNSTON:

Your command embraces the country west of the line between Georgia and Alabama, and running south to the Gulf; as, therefore, General Bragg's Department was formed, its western limit is the Mississippi river, and its northern boundary the Tennesse river and Kentucky line.

S. COOPER,
Adj't. and Inspector General.

(Official,)
BENJ. S. EWELL, *A. A. G.*